iLISTEN

:

God Speaks

<u>A Practical Guide To Hearing God's Voice</u>

Copyright © 2019 Kristen D. Baker

All rights reserved. No part of this book may be reproduced in any form or by an electronic or mechanical means, including information storage and retrieval systems, without permission in writing from the author, except by a reviewer who may quote brief passages in a review.

This book is dedicated to…

...a demographic I like to call the "churched-unchurched." Those that know who God is and love Him but don't go to church.

...Pastor Gary and Yasha Becton and the Revealing Word church family. You all will probably never know just how much your love and encouragement kept me from being the "churched-unchurched."

...to Mom, Dad, Bean, Jay, Rashad, and Kendrick, my amazing family and friends whose love and support is unmatched.

TABLE OF CONTENTS

Preface 1

Introduction 7

Chapter 1: Why God Speaks 17

Chapter 2: How God Speaks 25

Chapter 3: When God Speaks 65

Chapter 4: What God Speaks 77

Conclusion 87

Confessions and Affirmations 93

About the Author 99

PREFACE

The first book in my i3 series, a devotional titled *iHunger*, spoke practically on how to develop a closer walk with God. If you haven't read it, it's perfectly okay. This book is written to reach you *wherever* you are. This book speaks to what my Pastor, Yasha Becton, calls the four H's. Those that must come **h**ome, come **h**ere, come **h**onestly and come **h**igher.

Come Home

Many know the story of the prodigal son. The son that was so enamored with what he had not experienced or wanted to explore, more than being in the safety of "home." To be home is simply to be in relationship with God. There are a great many people who have come and left. Then came back home and left only to continue the cycle. If you can relate, this is for you. I am a realtor in South Carolina. Often when showing houses, you know a client has found *their* house when they can see themselves in it. Something that is brand new to you can and will feel like home. Whether you've been home and split or have *never* been home, this book is for you. In fact this book is *especially* for you.

Come Here

There are many people all over the world who confess to be a Christian. That word looks like different things to different people, but I can say this with absolute assurance, Jesus died for more than just your confession and earnestly desires closeness with you. As a little girl, I remember how affectionate my father was, (especially being a daddy's girl). He would summon me and then give me the best bear hugs and kisses. It didn't matter what I was doing when I heard him say, "Krrrriiiiiiissssss come here," almost as if he was singing it. I knew exactly what would happen next. What I need you to understand is that you may not "do church" like that, you may not pray like you should, you may not consistently read your Bible, but God is saying to you, "come here." If you're in a place where you have accepted God into your life, but have stopped there, this book is for you.

Come Honestly

So often in life we become so distracted by what and who other people are that we fashion our lives according to what they are doing. We do so at the expense of pursuing our own destiny and desires. There is no cookie-cutter way of living life, as some people may think. In trying to fit into certain crowds and molds, we often begin to lose the essence of who God made us. We put on facades and act as if everything is okay when it's not. We portray on social media that our lives are perfect, when they are not. We sing and preach things that we don't live. It is time to come to God honestly with who and where you are. Guess what? He already knows anyway.

1 John 1:19 says, "that *if we [freely] admit that we have sinned and confess our sins, He is faithful and just [true to His own nature and promises], and will forgive our sins and cleanse us continually from all unrighteousness [our wrongdoing, everything not in conformity with His will and purpose]*" (AMP). Now most religious people may have just thought "well I'm not sinning." However, I chose this version of scripture because I believe it expounded and covered all bases. So often when we think of "sin" we immediately go straight to sex, homosexuality/lesbianism, drugs and murder. However, we overlook what some would call "smaller sins" like gossip, idolatry, lying and pride. In fact, sin is also missing the mark. I miss God's mark much more often than I would like to admit and if you do too, this book is for you.

Come Higher

Acrophobia is the fear of heights. Fear because of the limitless possibilities. Fear of being alone away from everything and everyone that is familiar. Even fear of pain and dying. However, there are so many benefits of being "high." Not high as in high on drugs but high in perspective, proximity and productivity. I thought about the many experiences I've had riding a plane. The higher I am, the smaller things *behind* me become. The higher I am, the less obstacles obscure what's ahead of me. The higher I am, the better my perspective. It maybe a little lonely. It maybe a little painful. Your vision maybe just a little cloudy, but God is calling each of us *higher*. If you need to come up in your thinking, come up in your prayer life, come up in your kingdom productivity, this book is also for you.

Before we build a foundation for hearing God's voice, I want to set the expectation that if you are going to get to know God in a more real way, there is work for you to do. I know we always want everything to come easy. If you say you don't, then you're not telling the truth. No one really wants to, but in order to experience all that God has for you, you must learn to wait patiently. Why? Because God hides. Did you know that? **Isaiah 45:15** (NKJV) tells us, *"Truly You are God, who* **hide** *Yourself, O God of Israel, the Savior!"*

You may be wondering why God would hide himself, but think about it. Have you ever intentionally made yourself unavailable only to see what effort would be made to pursue you? How many times has the Bible talked about seeking God out? There is no need to **seek** what you can easily **see**. It would be incredibly rare or nearly impossible to find a precious jewel just laying around on the hot sand at your local beach. Treasures are to be sought after. I promise you with every fiber of my being that if you seek God with all your heart and wait patiently on Him you will not be disappointed. With Him comes a friend, father, guide, healer, protector, provider, saviour and everything you never even knew you needed!

Introduction

As believers in Christ, I believe we often live well below our privilege. God has equipped us with tools we must take full advantage of. One of the tools we often fail to use is the voice of God. You may wonder, *"Well, why doesn't God speak to me?"* What if God is speaking, but it's you that is not listening? I would even ask, *"What if God is speaking, but you don't recognize that it's Him?"* God told the prophet Elijah to go stand on the mountain because he was about to have a Divine encounter, (**I Kings 19:11-15**). The wind came and broke pieces of the mountain, but the Bible says that the Lord was not in the wind. An earthquake shook the foundation of where Elijah was standing, but the Lord was not in the earthquake. The fire came, but again God was not in the fire. After all of this, God in a still small voice spoke to Elijah. Often God speaking is associated with loudness and mighty wonders, but God speaks in so many ways. It is very important not to put God in a box or we run the risk of missing how, when and *what* He wants to say.

Sometimes in life, whether good or bad, we create routines for our lives. We have certain places we like to eat, certain things we do in the morning and certain traditions that we keep with our families. Many times, the first thing we do in the morning is look at our social media notifications or stop by our favorite coffee shop. But what if you made listening to God a habit? What would our lives be, if we made an obsession of hearing from God? I often wonder if we really understand the benefits of our amazing God. One of the *greatest* gifts God could have ever given to believers was the Holy Spirit. If you don't know where to go or what to do, the Spirit is a guide. If you're overwhelmed, He's a helper. If you're wounded or have experienced loss, He's a comforter. If you don't know something, the Spirit can teach you.

Jesus came to earth and turned it upside down with both His humanity and deity; challenging religion and man-made rules. He came, paid the ultimate cost by dying for our sins, but He had to leave earth in order to leave us Help. Oh how I wish I could have been with the disciples and those that walked closely with Him. While there is only one Jesus, when we accept Him into our lives, each one of us has access to the Holy Spirit. It doesn't matter whether you're a millennial like me, or if you are born 10 generations from now, each of us can be filled with the Holy Spirit.

I'm from the South and when we go over to someone's home, it is always proper to ask if there is anything that is needed. In fact, a good guest always brings a gift. I like to call the Spirit, my, "eternal guest." I want him to know He is always welcomed. Because of the Spirit residing in us, we then have access to the gifts that He brings, we refer to these as Spiritual Gifts.

1 Corinthians 12:6-11 (KJV)

*"**6** And there are diversities of operations, but it is the same God which worketh all in all. **7** But the manifestation of the Spirit is given to every man to profit withal. **8** For to one is given by the Spirit the word of wisdom; to another the word of knowledge by the same Spirit; **9** To another faith by the same Spirit; to another the gifts of healing by the same Spirit; **10** To another the working of miracles; to another prophecy; to another discerning of spirits; to another divers kinds of tongues; to another the interpretation of tongues: **11** But all these worketh that one and the selfsame Spirit, dividing to every man severally as he will."*

The nine gifts are...

1. Faith
2. Healing
3. Miracles
4. Tongues
5. Interpretation of Tongues
6. Discerning of Spirits
7. Word of Knowledge
8. Word of Wisdom

9. Prophecy

To gain an understanding about what, how, when and why God speaks, I think it is imperative that we further discuss the gifts of the word of knowledge, word of wisdom and prophecy. I often hear these gifts used interchangeably, but make no mistake about it, they are all different, yet very powerful gifts.

The word of knowledge is when God grants you access to information that you could not have known. The root word of knowledge is, "know," so, the word of knowledge is the Spirit giving you details that only He would know. Think about it, God is omnipresent. He is everywhere at the same time. He was in the past, is in the present and already is in the future. He knows because He is there to witness everything that happened and will happen. This spiritual gift is such an amazing tool because it gives us an explanation for what we have yet experienced. The word of knowledge will always deal with what has already happened, which also means that the word of knowledge will always be something that the receiver can verify. For example, after leaving my job to pursue my dreams and what God had given me to do, I spent the first few days working non-stop. I would work probably 10 to 12 hours a day because it was something very new to me. I was nervous even though I *knew* what God was telling me to do.

After spending more time with the Lord, I felt Him

nudging me to change my daily schedule. I was to spend more time with Him than I did working or at least as much time. I obeyed and began praying, meditating and studying the Word of God. Most days, I would look up and tell myself, *"Kris, you have not worked enough today."* I remember being at my church during a service and the speaker prayed for me. She said to me, *"I hear you saying you aren't working enough. I hear God saying that spending time with Me is your primary job right now."* I was literally floored because I had never actually uttered those words out of my mouth. This would be an example of a word of knowledge. It fits the description perfectly. 1.) I had never spoken it to anyone except to God in my head 2.) There was *no way* she could have known and 3.) I was able to confirm it.

The word of knowledge is often followed by the gift of the word of wisdom. The operative word in this gift speaks to its function: wisdom. This gift is one that gives instruction on how to move forward, handle, or accomplish what God has ordained. The word of wisdom will speak to what should be done in the future or what must continue being done. A word of wisdom is often used in conjunction with the word of knowledge in that it now gives you strategy to deal with what you know to be true. However, the word of wisdom can also be given apart from the word of knowledge as a solution to a problem or situation that the receiver may be dealing with.

An example is found in **John 21:1-6**. The disciples are

on the sea of Tiberias fishing all night. Jesus finds them and asks if they have caught any food (knowing full well that they had not). They answered, "no, we have caught nothing." Jesus then gives them a word of instruction on how to handle the current dilemma they are in. He tells them to switch gears and fish in the same boat, on the same sea, on the same day, but on a different side of the boat. As you may have already guessed or know, they caught more fish than they could handle. This is an example of a word of wisdom. It was a word of instruction on how to solve the problem they were facing.

Lastly, let's look at the gift of prophecy. I believe this is one of the most important spiritual gifts. The gift of prophecy embodies two concepts. First and most often talked about, is *foretelling*. To communicate what will take place in the future by the Spirit of God. "By the Spirit of God," is a very important part of the definition because it is the determining factor that differentiates a sorcerer or psychic from prophets and prophetic people. It is crucial that we know the source of the gifts that we possess. It is the Spirit of God, who is all-knowing, that gives us the power to unlock the future.

An example from the Bible is when the angel of the Lord comes to a young virgin who has never had intercourse and says, *"You will conceive in your womb and bring forth a Son, and shall call His name Jesus."* (**Luke**

1:31). Mary, was her name. This is one of the greatest examples of prophecy, because it points to the greatest miracle of all time: Jesus Christ! The second aspect of prophecy is forth-telling, which is establishing the will of God by declaration. When speaking for God, His thoughts, intentions and desires are being articulated. Moses is recorded as a prophet. Moses is widely known for leading the children of Israel out of the land of Egypt and His communication with God. Moses was tasked with regularly going on the mountain to talk with God and articulating what God had to say to the people. In fact, there was only one instance where God spoke to the people Himself, all other accounts are of Moses being the middleman by speaking for God. This too is an important aspect of prophecy.

I must be honest. There was a time in my life that my faith in the, "prophetic," was very low. In fact, it was almost non-existent. I had seen so much in ministry that it turned me off to perhaps some of the greatest tools God has given us; spiritual gifts. I have seen people abuse the gifts. I have seen prophets prophesy for profit only giving a prophetic word to the people in the, "$500 line," as if those with only $20 didn't need it or couldn't afford it. I have received words of knowledge that were just plain old wrong. I have seen and heard God, "say things," that the person found out through gossip or Facebook. I have even witnessed accurate words from God delivered with rudeness, grace-less and lacking in love.

I want to mention this because I believe that it's important, especially for those who have witnessed or experienced what I'm talking about. It is important to know this. The devil cannot create. He uses nothing new to distract us from being our God-ordained selves. However, He is a master at corruption. In other words, the enemy can't bring anything new to you, he can only corrupt that which God has already made. Anytime there is something counterfeit, what you can also be sure of, is that there has to be an authentic version somewhere. This is a challenge to you to start and/or continue being authentically, prophetically *you*.

It was important that before we go further that you understand each of these three gifts because when we talk about hearing God's voice, it will often be one or more of these. A word from the Lord is often lumped into the category of prophecy, when it may in fact be another gift in operation. Prophecy, I believe, is perhaps the greatest of all. What greater joy than to be able to hear God and speak on His behalf? After all, this is the gift of the spirit that Paul, the Gospel writer, put much emphasis on. He says in **1 Corinthians 14:1**(NKJV), *"Pursue love, and desire spiritual gifts, but <u>especially</u> that you may prophesy."*

While this scripture speaks to the importance of prophecy, it is also the basis of this entire book. God promised in **Psalm 37:4** that He would give us the desires of our hearts, if we delight ourselves in Him. If you don't remember anything before moving forward in this book remember this...it doesn't matter if you're a preacher. It doesn't matter where you're from. It doesn't matter where you've been or what you've done. You don't have to be a prophet to be prophetic. If you desire the gifts and delight yourself in Him, He will give you the desires of your heart. He *will* speak. Happy listening!

Oh wait… Here's a heads up on a few things before you officially start this journey. There will be times when I sound like the millennial, talking to a group of friends, but there will be other times I may come off slightly as the seminarian I am. However, I can assure you that everything written is inspired by God and sincere. Also I will use several versions of the Bible. There are some folk that think that King Jimmy, (King James Version), is king, but I wanted to use versions that would be easy to read and understandable. I did my best to give you a short, practical, yet inspiring work of literature. Seriously this time…Happy listening!

Chapter 1
Why God Speaks

From my perspective, it is hard to be a great father when you do not have a relationship with your children. Yes, provision is good. Buying pampers, school supplies and clothes are important, but children need something that money can't buy; and that is *time*. Time spent together. Time spent talking and getting to know each other. The same is true for us. God is our Heavenly Father and Creator. If you didn't already know, He is madly in love with you and thinks you're to die for. How could He not adore the masterpiece He made you to be? What awesome father is not consumed with unconditional love for his precious creation? None. It is the good pleasure of our Father to love and have a relationship with you.

God wants to have a relationship with each of us. And to take it a step further, He wants to have communion. Not communion in the sense of the wafer and little hard-to-open cup of grape juice, but fellowship. You may ask what is the difference? Think about it. I can be related to someone that I don't even know. How many people are you related to that you have not seen or talked to in ages? How many distant cousins do you have all over the world, that you don't even know or have never even seen before? I believe that before we surrender our lives to Christ, we are His creation, but not yet His children. When we allow God to be Lord of our lives, we are adopted into the royal family of God. Now that we are adopted, we have every right of a true son and daughter because of who our Father is.

The point I am making is that once we get saved, we become children of God, but it shouldn't stop there. If we don't make time to spend with God, we will never take full advantage of all that Jesus died for. One of the most important aspects of any relationship is COMMUNication. The more you speak to a person, the more you get to know them. You remember your first boyfriend or girlfriend, right? Do you remember how your heart smiled when you saw them calling? Being so in love, (or at least, "in like"), that you were willing to talk even 'til the late hours of the night or early morning. You remember not wanting to hang up and even falling asleep on the phone together.

It was in constant fellowship where you learned their likes and dislikes, wants and desires, what makes them happy or angry. You learned about their past, present and future ambitions. My prayer is that you develop this type of relationship with God. I don't know about you, but I want to be so in love with Him that He's the last person I think about when I lay down and the first person I think about when my feet hit the floor in the morning. I want to be so in love, that I miss when we don't talk. So in love that I won't make any decisions without talking to Him about it.

Prayer is the way we build this type of relationship and communicate with God. As a teenager, I learned a formula for prayer called **A.C.T.S.**, which stands for **a**doration, **c**onfession, **t**hanksgiving and **s**upplication. Adoration is to give praise and glory to God for all He is and all He has done. **Psalm 100:4** says that we should enter His gates with thanksgiving and into His courts with praise. Gates and courts typically surround the temple where God's presence dwells, which leads me to believe that praise and thanksgiving should precede everything we do, *especially* in prayer. Confession is simply that, to confess. As we attempt to enter God's presence, we should confess our sins and faults to Him (**1 John 1:9**). He is faithful to forgive us and cleanse us from all unrighteousness. We should follow David's example in **Psalm 51:10**, when he said, *"Create in me a clean heart O God and renew a right spirit in me."*

Then as we pray to God from our hearts, we are praying from a sincere and pure place. I often use thanksgiving twice in my prayer time. I first thank and praise God for all He has done. This is important because when you are building a relationship with someone, you don't want to always be asking for something, nor do you want to receive from them without ever thanking them. I believe the same should be true for God. In fact, I often have days where I don't ask for anything. I thank Him for everything. Secondly, I use thanksgiving after I have prayed specifically for my needs and the needs of others. I thank God after I have petitioned Him for needs to show that I have trust not only in His ability to do what has been asked, but also in His willingness to meet the need, be it natural or spiritual.

Lastly, is supplication. I have kinda already given it away, but supplication is prayer to God for your needs and the needs of others. This is not to say that every prayer is the same whether in length, location, or style, but I believe there are elements that should be present in your prayer time. There is one key element that is often missing from our prayer life and that is listening. We say that prayer is communication with the Father, but communication is a two-way street. Have you ever thought about the fact that we often get up from prayer, giving God all our cares and concerns, but never give Him the opportunity to respond? I don't know about you, but when I meet someone and all they want to talk about is themselves, I wonder if the relationship will even work. What am I saying? Is a monologue or one-sided talk really communication? If we are to engage in effective communication with God, we must listen just as much as we speak. In my first book, *iHunger*, I called it a, "daily exchange." To exchange means to give one thing and receive another. Give your cares, concerns, needs and requests to God, but also allow yourself to be a ready recipient.

There is something that I have always wondered about. If God created everything in seven days, (and He did), what is He in Heaven doing? I submit to you that God is simply watching over His Word to bring it to pass, (**Jeremiah 1:12**). God is the self-existent One. He is a timeless being. God existed before time began. He exists without time. He does not exist at *any point* in time, rather at every point in time. He is the Creator of time and I believe that God created time as a delivery service, like Uber, if you will. Because God did and said all He would say before we were even in our mother's womb, He simply used time to deliver the words that had already been spoken. So to us God *is* speaking, when in reality God has spoken.

Do you remember learning about Abraham and Isaac in Sunday School? See **Genesis 22:1-18**, and if not, here's the short version. Abraham was an old man. In fact he was a *very* old man. He was 100 years old to be exact, when God promised Abraham and his wife, Sarah, that they would conceive a son. Sarah laughed like, "God, yeah right. I'm too old for that," but sure enough Sarah bore a son named Isaac. When Isaac grew into a young lad, God tells Abraham to go up on the mountain and sacrifice Isaac. Yep, God tells Abraham to kill the very thing He promised him in the first place. Abraham being such a friend and lover of God, obeys Him. He starts the journey and Isaac says, *"Wayment Dad, where's the animal for the sacrifice?"*

Abraham tells him don't worry about it. God will make

a way. They finally get to the mountain and before Abraham could slay Isaac, the angel of God stops him and tells him not to kill Isaac, but to slay the ram that was caught in the bush. Why is this story important? It teaches some very good lessons. We are talking about daily spending time with God in prayer and the scriptures right? What if Abraham listened to the first instruction, but not the second? Where would Isaac be had Abraham heard God say sacrifice him, but not to spare him? It is important not just to hear what God said, (past tense), but to hear what God is saying, (present tense).

Many times, we are inconsistent in our pursuit of God, but also worry about ambiguity and uncertainty in our lives. Our lack of direction is often directly related to our lack of devotion. We must take the stance of David in **Psalms 1:2-3** (Voice) when he said,

For you, the Eternal's Word is your happiness. It is your focus—from dusk to dawn. You are like a tree, planted by flowing, cool streams of water that never run dry. Your fruit ripens in its time; your leaves never fade or curl in the summer sun. No matter what you do, you prosper.

One attribute I love about God is that He is all knowing; He knows every hair on your head. He knows what you did last summer. He knows your deepest thoughts. He knows the past, present and future. I don't know about you, but for me it is often hard to know certain things about people. It takes love and maturity to know the worst about people and still love them to their best. What I love about God, is that He knows our deepest darkest secrets and still loves us. He cares for us so much that He would even share pertinent information. God speaks so that we know the future.

I believe that if there is something we as the body of Christ do not know, someone wasn't paying attention. The Holy Spirit, among many things, is a teller and a teacher according to **John 14:26**. He will tell you what you need to know and teach you what you don't already know. In a world of such uncertainty this is imperative for the believer. Why live in uncertainty when your Father knows everything? You don't have to! He wants to give you instruction and direction. Set aside some time to hear what God is speaking to you.

Please understand that listening to God is a spiritual discipline. If you're like me, sometimes you become still to pray or read and you begin to think about things you need to get done, what happened to you today or even fall asleep. Just like exercising or dieting, sometimes you get off track and eat cookies and cream ice cream. Sometimes you only do 25 crunches when you could really push yourself to 50. Maybe you skipped the gym to go see a movie, but anyone who is committed will do everything they can to get back on track. The same is true for your spiritual disciplines. You may mess up, but remember there's grace for that!

Chapter 2
How God Speaks

God speaks in many ways. It is important for us to know *how* He speaks so that we are able to recognize *when* He speaks. You may ask, how do I know when God is speaking? Jesus says that my sheep follow me and know my voice, and a stranger they will not follow, (**John 10:4-5**). You will begin to know God's voice, the more you spend time with Him. Recently, a friend of my family called me from her work phone. I answered, only to not recognize her voice in the first greeting, (people tend to talk differently while they're at work than in these streets lol). She never announced who she was, but as she began to continue talking, I recognized her voice, even with the work phone tone.

Now this is someone who my family has known for years. We have been to many events together. Been to church together. We have been to each other's family functions many times. Because of the fellowship that we have, even though she spoke a little differently I was still able to distinguish her voice. The same is true for our relationship with God. The more time we spend in His presence; the more we talk to Him, the better we are at recognizing His voice. Recognition comes with relationship. As forestated, God speaks in many ways, and even if He speaks in a way that differs from how He has spoken before, we will still know its Him.

God Speaks Through The Word of God

One of the surest ways to know what God has said and is saying, is through His Word. **John 1:1** says, *"In the beginning was the Word, and the Word was with God, and the Word was God."* God is His very Word. The Word of God is the very ruler by which we should measure life's decisions and accomplishments. If in no other way, God is speaking to each and every one of us through His Word. It is the Word of God that is the basis of everything God will say through the other ways in which He speaks. You will never be very familiar with God's voice if you are not first engrossed in His Word. As discussed in chapter 1, the closer you become to someone, the more you recognize their voice.

In addition to learning *the* voice, you also begin to learn character. It is the Word of God that helps us understand and uncover God's character; they way He feels, what and how He thinks. I remember going through some *very* public scrutiny. All types of allegations and opinions were being shared based on a post from a social media bully hiding behind a fake page. People began to treat me differently. Some distanced themselves. Others begrudgingly spoke or greeted me. Very few reached out to say anything, let alone pray or encourage me. I struggled with publicly speaking about it or if I would keep silent and ride it out. Before making any bold move, I seek wise counsel.

On one hand, I could look guilty if I didn't address it and on the other I would bring even more attention to it and look guilty if I further entertained it publicly. This was a time where I really should have sought God's opinion, but I was just in a place... Have you ever been in a place where you're so torn and in so much pain it's hard to pray? Yea, that's where I was. It was one of the hardest things I've ever had to endure, but I realized something. I realized that the people closest to me never changed. They walked with me, covered me in prayer and never questioned my innocence or guilt. Why? Simply because they were close enough to know my character. It is important to know God's Word, especially when you are learning His voice. As God speaks to you, and through others, what is spoken must always align with what He has already said. Take a moment to read this story of Jesus and the devil and we'll come back and talk about it.

Satan Tempts Jesus- Luke 4:1-13

"4 Then Jesus, being filled with the Holy Spirit, returned from the Jordan and was led by the Spirit into the wilderness, 2 being tempted for forty days by the devil. And in those days He ate nothing, and afterward, when they had ended, He was hungry.

3 And the devil said to Him, "If You are the Son of God, command this stone to become bread."

4 But Jesus answered him, saying, "It is written, 'Man shall not live by bread alone, but by every word of God.' "

5 Then the devil, taking Him up on a high mountain, showed Him all the kingdoms of the world in a moment of time. 6 And the devil said to Him, "All this authority I will give You, and their glory; for this has been delivered to me, and I give it to whomever I wish. 7 Therefore, if You will worship before me, all will be Yours."

8 And Jesus answered and said to him, "Get behind Me, Satan! For it is written, 'You shall worship the Lord your God, and Him only you shall serve.' "

9 Then he brought Him to Jerusalem, set Him on the pinnacle of the temple, and said to Him, "If You are the Son of God, throw Yourself down from here. 10 For it is written:

'He shall give His angels charge over you,

To keep you,'

11 and,

'In their hands they shall bear you up,

Lest you dash your foot against a stone.' "

12 And Jesus answered and said to him, "It has been said, 'You shall not tempt the Lord your God.' "

13 Now when the devil had ended every temptation, he departed from Him until an opportune time."

This story is so loaded, I'm going to try and refrain from going into "preacher mode" and stick to the topic at hand (lol). First, there is one point this story brings up that also speaks to the foundation of this entire book. Jesus said to the devil, *"It is written, 'Man shall not live by bread alone, but by every word of God."* We must hear God. Food is good and necessary for our natural bodies, but the Word of God is a necessity for your spiritual well-being. Peter told us that we should desire the sincere milk of the Word of God, so that we may grow. In order to mature in the things of God, we must consume the Word of God daily, (**1 Peter 2:2**). You should only pray and read the Word of God on the days that you eat, (which for the majority of us is everyday multiple times a day).

It is also important to note that though we often get off track, the enemy is always on his job. The end of this story tells us that He left for a while, but that we would be back when the time was right. Rest assured as there is breath in your body, we will have an adversary on our trail, especially if we are doing all we can to follow God. This is all the more reason why we should daily immerse ourselves in Scripture. **Ephesians 6** tells us to be dressed in the whole armor of God. That includes the sword of the Spirit, which is the Word of God. You can't fight without it. You can't win without it! Here's a catch though. The devil knows the word. In the story referenced above, he uses scripture to try and throw Jesus off His game, but you find that Jesus throws the Word right back at him.

The enemy is a master manipulator and will mix truth and lies to present a compelling case as to why you should disobey God- ask Adam and Eve (**Genesis 3:1-7**). The Bible actually says that in the final days, even the most elect, God's chosen ones, may be deceived as a result of his tactics (**Matthew 24:24**). Understand that the enemy will always try and taint anything God has said or done. This again is why we must know the Word and character of God. When the enemy tells you that you won't make it or that you should just give up on life or when He tells you God didn't say what you know He said, you will have proof in the Word of God. When you get a word of prophecy that does not align with the Word of God, you will know that it is not from God. Again, God will never contradict His Word. He will never say anything to you that goes against what He has already said in His Word. This is the importance of the Word of God.

God Speaks Through Dreams and Visions

A few years ago I started a journey on knowing more about the supernatural. Now, don't get scared or spooked on me. I'm not talking about witches or ghosts. The supernatural I am referring to is simply God gifting our natural man His super divine abilities. Get it? Super + natural = supernatural. The supernatural is another way of talking about the gifts of the spirit we have already discussed. Anyway, I began the journey about two years ago. I started reading books on the prophetic and spiritual gifts, watching preaching and teaching on it, and asking lots of questions. One of the most important things I could have done was desire to operate in the gifts. **1 Corinthians 14:1** says

"To pursue love [with eagerness, make it your goal], yet earnestly desire and cultivate the spiritual gifts [to be used by believers for the benefit of the church], but especially that you may prophesy [to foretell the future, to speak a new message from God to the people]."

It was because of my desire and hunger, that the Lord began to deal with me prophetically through dreams and visions. The Scripture is clear that what will start to happen is that young men shall see visions. Let me first address the fact that if you're reading this and don't consider yourself to be "young," it's okay. You're not excluded. The same Scripture in the book of Joel, is also clear that God would pour out His spirit upon, not just young flesh, not just older flesh, but *all* flesh. It is also important to understand that both visions and dreams can be prophecy and/or they can give you a word of knowledge or word of wisdom. There are so many possibilities in the spirit realm. Let's take a further look.

What is a vision? My personal definition of a vision is a method of revelation supernaturally articulated in the form of a picture or a moving picture while you are conscious. A vision could be of absolutely anything God wants to show you. There are two types of visions; closed visions and open visions. Closed visions are the most prevalent of the two. A closed vision is typically a vision when your eyes are closed, but you are awake. An example of a vision is shown in the **Amos 8:1**(NLT).

*"Then the Sovereign Lord showed me another vision. In it I saw a basket filled with ripe fruit. Amos also speaks of another vision in **Amos 7:1** that says The Sovereign Lord showed me a vision. I saw him preparing to send a vast swarm of locusts over the land. This was after the king's share had been harvested from the fields and as the main crop was coming up."*

Amos saw a picture of what God wanted to tell him to tell the people. The second of which appears to be a moving picture, showing the swarm of locusts. This again gives only two of many examples of visions in the Bible.

The visions I have seen have all taken place in my quiet time with the Lord. This again is a time that you intentionally carve space out to give to God. This does not mean that this is the only time you will see visions, but as previously discussed, we are often too busy to notice when God is speaking, unless we slow down long enough to receive what He wants to give us. I remember receiving a closed vision and thinking, "Now God..." It was nothing I had ever thought of or even wanted to do. I saw a vision of some of my family members around a table having a meeting. At the time, there was some conflict that I would rather not be apart of. So here I was being called upon to get right in the middle of it. I was obedient. Though the family meeting didn't turn out the way I had planned, it certainly gave me a perspective I had not previously seen. What it did was position me to pray a different prayer concerning the situation, which was huge for me.

I will be completely transparent with you. I have seen some visions of me slapping the hell out of a few people! (Didn't see that coming, right)? No, really it's true though. Sometimes it's simply daydreaming; self-initiated visions. I've seen visions of things I knew weren't Godly. What am I saying? I'm saying be careful of, "soulish" visions. Soulish visions come from the seat of your soul. Remember what the soul houses: your feelings, your will and your emotions. Visions from God will never inspire you to act outside of God's character. And I'm not sure you can say that I slapped someone in the name of Jesus, (although I'm sure you, like me, have been tempted to do so a time or 10).

Soulish visions are not to be disregarded. They highlight something that has happened, or is happening that you need to deal with. As aforementioned, you must make sure alignment with the Word of God and the purpose of

God is accompanied with what you feel He's saying. Until you have first measured the spirituality of what you have to say, keep your mouth closed. But never minimize the value of what you see.

An open vision or trance is a vision you see with your eyes open. Open visions tend to appear as if you are an onlooker at a real-life 3D movie right in front of you. I once read an article and love the way the author explains it. He said, *"...when a man has an open vision of an angel like in Acts 10, he will see the angel in relation to his own physical surroundings so his natural senses are not suspended, he is aware of where he is, but still sees into the spirit realm."* This type of vision is quite rare, but certainly not impossible. Actually much of the Book of Revelation is an account of John describing what will happen in the last days from an open vision.

Revelation 1:1 (Voice) sets the stage for the entire book. It says, *"This is the revelation of Jesus the Anointed, the Liberating King: an account of visions and a heavenly journey. God granted this to Him so He would show His followers the realities that are already breaking into the world and soon will be fulfilled. Through His heavenly messenger, He revealed to His servant John signs and insight into."* I challenge you to read the book of Revelation. Look at the visions that John had and how they affect us to this day. The King James Version can be difficult to comprehend, but find a version that works for you and read it. It will blow your mind.

Joel 2:28 (Voice)

*"Then in those days I will pour My Spirit to all humanity; your children will boldly and prophetically speak **(prophesy)** the word of God. Your elders will dream **dreams**; your young warriors will see **visions**."*

This scripture in Joel brings to light that prophecy, dreams and visions are the inheritance of the saints. Notice that I said inheritance. In the physical realm, you only gain an inheritance when someone dies, right? You may have figured out where I'm going with this. Jesus died specifically for our sins and in turn gave us the right and freedom to be filled and endowed with the Helper, who is the Holy Ghost. So all men and women, whether young or old, have a right to the gifts of the Spirit. We've talked about visions, and we've touched on prophecy. Now let's talk about dreams. I honestly couldn't wait to get to this part. This is how God primarily speaks to me in this season of my life.

I define a prophetic dream as a method of revelation supernaturally articulated in the form of a picture or series of pictures while you are asleep. Dreams are also known as visions of the night, or night visions, (See Daniel 7). Everyone dreams. You may be thinking, "not me," but scientifically, everyone who has a fully functioning brain, dreams. Studies have shown that every person dreams from one to two hours a night. In fact, after about 90 minutes of sleep you enter into what is called R.E.M. You may remember from science class that REM is Rapid Eye Movement. This is the stage of sleep where dreaming takes place.

When I think of REM I see a picture of an old time movie reel. Have you ever heard its sound? The clicking sound of each picture quickly moving to create a captivating story. It is a picture of exactly what happens in the rapid eye movement stage as we dream. Scientists still don't have a grasp on why we dream, but God often defies science. The difference between a regular dream and a prophetic dream, is that a prophetic dream comes directly from God. Most dreams you forget as soon as you wake up. Prophetic dreams are more likely to be remembered. Some are even etched in the memory of your mind.

In ancient times, dreams were viewed as supernatural so much so that they were either feared, or sought after because of the magnitude of revelation that accompanied dreams from God. Many sought after and employed dream interpreters to uncover the meaning of their dreams. For example, both Daniel and Joseph were dreamers and interpreters of dreams. Daniel volunteered to interpret the dream of King Nebuchadnezzar and found favor with him. Joseph was summoned to interpret the dreams of Pharaoh and found favor with him. These two men were vital to the times they lived in because the dreams that they interpreted, were about the future of things that would directly affect them and the entire earth. These Kings realized that the dreams could only be interpreted with the help of the one true and living God.

When God opened up this gift to me, I began to become even more intrigued and to study dreams; symbols, numbers and colors. While this book isn't solely about dreams, I want to share a few things that I've learned and experienced.

- The dreams I am referring to come straight from the throne of God. For the sake of differentiation, let's call them God-dreams.
- Dreamers are seers, which simply means they see revelation, (go figure). A picture really is worth a thousand words.
- First natural, then spiritual. God can't speak to you in dreams if you're not getting ample rest. Selah.
- There are three categories of dreams. Dreams that come from 1. God 2. You (soul) and 3. The devil.
- Just like there are "soulish" visions, there are soulish dreams. Similar to the visions, they have to do with something in your soul, (feelings, desires, emotions), that need some spiritual attention. For example, if you dream of having sex with someone and you're not married and/or it's not your spouse, "Houston we have a problem." Any message from God will lead you to God, not away from Him nor His will.
- In my experience, God-dreams will often happen just before I wake up. I am thankful for this because it is fresh and helps me to remember it long enough

to write it down. You are often only one thought away from forgetting what you have seen. In fact, most nights I pray that God would speak to me as I sleep and help me to remember that which is important to Him.

- Dreams that are in black and white are usually, if not always from the enemy. God-dreams will always be in color. Color represents beauty, light and life. All characteristics of God and our life with Him. If you have a black and white dream, there is something wrong spiritually and it needs attention.

- Your reactive feeling to the dream often speaks to the nature or interpretation of it. For example, I had a dream about one of my cousins. My family was all at a hospital because we heard that someone with the same name had been hurt. I awakened with my heart rate escalated, nervous and scared. After praying, I discerned that this was a call to action to intercede for him. The same dream without my physical reaction would not have given me the same concern.

- Literal dreams (and visions) that show the exact meaning. And there are symbolic dreams that must be interpreted. I believe that literal dreams are often time-sensitive. Symbolic dreams sometimes take days, weeks and even years to get the full revelation. If that is the case, why would God give you a complex symbolic dream that may take time to pray about and interpret and you need to

intercede on someone's behalf in an emergency?
- For example, if you have a dream that you are preaching, (a destiny dream), chances are this dream is not a puzzle. It is highly likely that you will or should be preaching. On the other hand, let's say you have a dream that it's storming and you're not sure where to go. Your father picks you up in his silver car and takes you to your destination on 8th Street. Storms typically represent trials. Father is often symbolic of the Father. Silver is symbolic of grace or redemption. Eight is the number of new beginnings. Maybe God is telling you that He knows you've been in a season of trials and tribulations and you just don't know where to turn. He is telling you that His grace will carry you where you need to go; a place of new beginnings and a new start.
- There are also internal and external dreams. Internal dreams are about the dreamer. Whereas external dreams are about someone else or an event.
- You know this dream is not about you when you are an observer, not a participant. Even if you are a participant, be sure to determine whether you have a starring role or if you are an extra. This will give insight into whether or not the dream is about you or someone else.
- Act on your dreams. Pray, move forward, start something, have a conversation; do *something*. The Holy Spirit is a helper and teacher *in* all things, but

not a doer *of* all things. In other words, the Holy Spirit will not do everything for you. What He wants to do in and through will do will require your effort. Dreams are a call to action even if the action is only to pray.

- The most practical interpretation is probably the correct one. Be sure, however, to bathe the interpretation in prayer.

I have had dreams about myself and quite a bit about other people. I have had dreams about people starting new jobs and getting fired from jobs. I have dreams about people dying and babies being born. I have dreams about celebrities, suicide, marriages, preaching, songs, all *kinds* of things. When I'm focused, get enough rest, and consistent in my devotion, I dream maybe every two to four days. Now let me clarify because I think many of you will relate to exactly what I'm about to say. When I say consistent in my devotion, please understand that I pray everyday. I mean *consistent* in devotion, deep communion with God.

I don't mean you leave home and pray on your 10-minute drive to work. Now don't get me wrong. God is sovereign. He can do anything, at any time, anyway He wants to. However, I am encouraging you to carve out time that is His and only His. Time that does not have to compete with social media, or your family, or anything else that will distract you. The type of relationship we are striving to have and/or maintain with God is going to take time and consistency. It's funny because I sometimes look at my journal with all my dreams, (which we'll talk later about). There are a few big gaps. I can pinpoint the times that I have gotten off track. I can also tell when I get back on track because the dreams are pretty consistent. I want to talk about a few dreams and then I'll tell you why I'm telling you what I'm telling you.

I've kinda touched on how I really lost faith in myself and everyone else. I distanced myself from everyone and everything. I battled several years with depression and most people didn't even know. I saw little to no value in myself nor in the gifts God had given me. And one day out of the blue, I get a Facebook message. At the time I didn't really know the person and was like, "Oh Lord, here comes a Facebook prophet." So I honestly didn't rush to open the message. My pastor then texts me and says hey, "Pastor Chicken Wings" had a dream about you and sent it on Facebook. Because my pastor told me to, I went to see what the dream was about and this is what she said. "Last night in a dream God said to me concerning you... You are a KINGDOM GEM. He showed me a very large diamond housed in clear case, set on a stand and protected by velvet ropes and a security guard. YOUR KINGDOM VALUE WARRANTS FULL SECURITY. The Angels of the Lord are encamped around you. Be blessed as you keep doing what God has called you to do. Many blessings for your day!" Now, mind you, I received this message at this point where I was better than I was, but still not thinking of myself how the way God sees me. I literally just started crying again reading this because it still amazes me howGod knows exactly what you need when you need it. And it's not just for me. You too, are a gem; the apple of His eye.

I've learned that relationships can make or break you. So much so, that one of the things that I started praying about are my connections. In *iHunger,* I talked about how connections determine the strength of your power. I began to pray specifically about the people in my life and whether or not they should be there. I also believe that there are people who are assigned to you and at this point in my life, those are the relationships that I fight to keep. Everyone else can be blessed on their way, anywhere else. You *must* protect your peace and your purpose.

I remember having such a vivid dream it still tickles me. I had a dream that one of the people was talking about me behind my back. To be honest, this wasn't really a shock, I guess I had an inner knowing. However what shocked me is the other person in the text thread. I wasn't praying about him nor was he on my radar at all, but I was thankful for the inside scoop. I mean y'all I could see the texts so clear. Clear enough to see that whoever's phone I was looking into had an Android. (I don't even like those green messages. We're "Applestolic" in this here church). Seriously though, I'll never forget waking up like, "Hmmm thanks for the confirmation God."

I woke up, prayed and acted accordingly. Out of all the dreams I've had since I started this journey, I thought this was important. Not so I can brag about seeing it or gossip to other people. It is important because it speaks to the fact that if you seek God, He will reveal the secrets of men's hearts. He is a shepherd and will often expose wolves disguised as sheep to protect you even if it hurts. In addition to that, God is so concerned about who you are connected to. **Psalm 1:1** reminds us *"God's blessings follow you and await you at every turn: when you don't follow the advice of those who delight in wicked schemes, When you avoid sin's highway, when judgment and sarcasm beckon you, but you refuse."* There is a blessing in being connected to the right people.

Another dream that sticks out to me is one I had about someone who I haven't seen or talked to in years and lives in a whole 'nother state. I had a dream that this person was sitting with me at what appeared to be a school. She was helping me with life changes like saving money and building wealth. She told me her personal story and her journey to financial freedom. I woke up, "Like God that was whack. You got anything better?" No, but seriously. Because the dream was not as juicy or adventurous as others, I mistakenly saw it as insignificant. I almost didn't even tell the person about the dream. But I felt a nudge to share the dream, so I did. At this point, my dreams had been so on point that I was confident that if I dreamt it, it already happened or it was sure to happen.

I got a little nervous because it took her *so* long to respond. Once she finally did, this was her response. "The way I've had to read this 3x today... this is a private prayer revealed by the Prophet...I am thankful! You just don't know! It's time to level UP! God bless you for the release of this." First I had a sigh of relief that I didn't just put my neck on the line only to be wrong. Once that feeling was gone, I had to repent. I promised God that day that no matter what He showed me or how insignificant I thought it was, I would start valuing everything I hear and see. Why? Because whatever He does and says is worthy of my attention.

I want to address one more thing before we go to the next way that God speaks. I remember being at a Bible study of my youth pastor, who is currently my pastor. The topic, I believe, was about purpose and who God called you to be. Everyone had to stand up in courage and say what God has made you. I remember being prophesied to and having an inner knowing since I was a young girl, but I was still gripped with fear, (and to some extent still to this day). It was my turn to share and I wanted to run out and take a fake phone call. I put my big girl boots on stood up literally trembling and sweating and said, "I'm a prophet." In all honesty, I really struggle with being called that. If you're like me and that title completely terrifies you, I want to tell you this, You are what God has made you. Period. Never let people put undue pressure on you to be anything else, but what He's called you to be. We often get caught up and discouraged at the fact that we are not where someone else it but please understand that you have to start somewhere. When I was a little girl I used to hear the mothers of the church sing a song that said "God uses ordinary people...little becomes much when you place it in the master's hand." Use what you have with excellence and consistency and God will increase you.

One of the reasons is because I hate when people ask, "What is the Lord saying?" On one hand He should be saying something, but on the other hand I want to reply, "What is He saying to you ma'am/sir?" What I do believe is that if we take the pressure off of you and put it on the all-knowing One, He will do what needs to be done. Trust Him! This is also no pressure to anyone who may not have the gift of prophecy. You don't have to be a prophet to prophesy. Again Paul said in **1 Corinthians 14:1** to pursue love and desire the gifts of the spirit *especially* prophecy. If you desire the gift, make your request known and seek it out. This has not even scratched the surface of dreams and dream interpretation, but I hope you are becoming more intrigued about the gifts and hungry for more of God.

As wonderful as spiritual gifts are and as exhilarating as it is to know that we can ask for AND receive them, I would be remiss if I did not admonish you. Don't, I repeat, do not place the gift over the Giver. Seeking spiritual gifts without first seeking intimacy with God is imminently dangerous to your spirit man, your soul and your destiny.

I'm sure that's not what you want. It's my sincere prayer that you fall in love with God for who He is and not just because He is the giver of gifts.

God Speaks Through the Inner Witness, Knowings and "Divine Halts"

First, I think it is important to understand that we as humans are triune beings. "Tri" meaning three. What that simply means is that we are made of three parts. Similar to an egg which has the shell, the egg white and the yolk. It also mirrors the makeup of the Trinity. Just how the Father, Son and Holy Spirit are one, we are made up of spirit, soul and body. Genesis 2:7 shows us how God created man, *"then the Lord God formed [that is, created the body of] man from the dust of the ground, and breathed into his nostrils the breath of life; and the man became a living being [an individual complete in body and spirit]."* God forms the *body* of man. Then breathes the breath or *spirit* of life into the man. Then man becomes a living *soul*.

So to sum it up, we are spirit. We have a soul and live in a body. The body is the physical earth suit which we wear everyday. The body gives us access to the physical world. This is the seat of our senses; how we touch, see, smell, hear and taste. Our bodies, whether short or tall, plump or skinny, black or white, are the temporal part of us. The part that dies and is buried back in the dust from where we came. This is not to say our bodies are not as important as the other components. After all, it is our body that is the temple of the Holy Spirit and should be valued as such (1 Corinthians 6:19). Second is the soul. The soul is the seat of our emotions, will, intellect and personality. The soul is the part of us that speaks to who we really are and what we desire, how we act and react. Most importantly, our spirit is how we were made in God's image. He breathed His spirit into each of us.

Our spirits give us access to the spiritual realm and the means by which we have faith in God, give worship to God and communicate with God as a result of our salvation. There are several things that happen when you get saved. I'm not sure if we covered this and want to explain for anyone who may not know what it means. To be saved simply means to be forgiven of sin and *saved* from eternal condemnation and punishment. To be saved, is to experience a spiritual rebirth. It was Adam and Eve's sin that caused us to live according to our own fleshly desires instead of according to the spirit. Our spirits then became slaves to our carnal desires instead of the other way around. Our lustful, worldly desires to be famous, full of ourselves, filthy rich, and "fast" is a direct result of the spiritual death that took place in, "the fall of man" (Genesis 3). It was always God's will for us to live in the Spirit, walk in the Spirit, play in the Spirit: whatever we did it was to be done in the Spirit. Because of sin, we were separated from God and now live our lives to be redeemed back to Him as He originally intended.

It is important for us to understand that while we all

are spirit beings, it is up to us to operate in *the* spirit, the spirit of God. That fact is true, that whoever you feed will be the strongest. You can feed your flesh or you can feed your spirit. Many times, we feed off of television, social media, gossip, non-spiritual music and wonder why our spirits are weak. I challenge you to make time daily for spiritual nourishment. Take in the word of God, worship, fellowship with other believers and prayer. You will be amazed by how strong you grow in the Spirit and how sensitive you become to God's voice. In fact, one of the ways you will know if you are God's child, is if He leads you. Romans 8:14 says, *"That if the Spirit of God is leading you, then take comfort in knowing you are His children."* (Voice). It is our spirit that allows us to connect with the Holy Spirit. *The Spirit Himself testifies and confirms together with our spirit [assuring us] that we [believers] are children of God (Romans 8:16 AMP).*

Many times in the legal system, the prosecution or defense, calls a witness to testify to, or confirm, what is being presented to the court. The same is true for the spirit that dwells within you, which brings me to another way God speaks. One of the most prevalent ways God speaks, aside from His Word, is through our inner witness. The spirit within you will agree and bear witness to the Spirit of God. Only spirit can connect and agree with spirit. Have you ever experienced this inner knowing? That feeling in the pit of our stomach that you just *knew* something without a shadow of a doubt that you didn't really know?

The feeling of knowing something that may or may not make any sense at all. This also goes back to the introduction about the gifts of the spirit. The word of knowledge, knowing information that you could not possibly know or the gift of the word of wisdom, which is words of instruction on how to handle a situation or solve a problem. Some people may call it intuition or a gut feeling, but you have to be careful with those. They can sometimes come from your soul, the seat of your emotions. The more you experience the inner witness, the more sure you become when the Holy Spirit speaking.

You can recognize an inner witness by pieces of information that are not self-induced or self-initiated. Sometimes we can think up things that we feel or want, but the inner witness, in my experience, will often give information that I am not seeking at the moment. This is also why it is important to have specific times when you do nothing, but listen to God in a quiet place with a notebook. I can't stress enough that there should be a time where we are intentional about giving the Holy Spirit space to speak to us.

Another way you can recognize an inner knowing is when it just won't leave you alone. It keeps coming up, whether in your spirit, thoughts or by an outside source. I often either see faces while I'm in prayer or just think about people I don't talk to on a regular basis. I have found that nine point nine nine times out of ten, they needed someone to reach out to them. Recently, a former church member was on my mind. I had intended to reach out to them, but kept forgetting. One morning in prayer, I can't remember if I saw their face or if they just came up in my thoughts, but I remember stopping what I was doing to contact them right at that moment, because it had been about the third time they had come up in my spirit. I texted him that morning at 7:56 am, (not thinking he would even respond that early), "Brother! U were on my mind. Pray all is well. Please tell your wife I said hello! Love you all."

He replied, "Man you are in the spirit. I had been battling spiritual warfare mentally." I knew exactly what he meant and that this could not have been haphazard, (characterized by lack of order or planning, by irregularity, or by randomness; determined by or dependent on chance; aimless). Now, this is someone who I hadn't seen or talked to in about eight months at that point. And there was absolutely no way that I could know at that very moment that he needed to know that He was on God's mind!

Another way you can recognize an inner knowing is that it is accompanied by a feeling of unexplainable peace. This may sound small, but never underestimate the power of peace. When making a major decision, I *always* consult other people. Whether my pastor, parents or friends. I always seek wise counsel, emphasis on wise, (Proverbs 19:20). More importantly though, I have learned to not only get wise counsel, but to give the Holy Spirit space to give a green, yellow, or red light. This green light is that feeling of unexplainable peace with a decision. The yellow light can be one we may not like, but is sometimes what God wants and the best thing for us. The yellow light is the, "not yet."

I appreciate the yellow light as well as the others because it speaks to God's timing. Like the saying goes, "Timing is *everything*." God's timing, I have found, is impeccable. Have you ever looked at your life as something that really hurt or upset you, but looked back and THANKED GOD it didn't happen!? It is a beautiful thing. The voice of God communicates the timing of God. Know this...the wrong thing is always wrong, but even the right thing can become wrong in the wrong time. Trust God's voice to know the right time to start a business, or the right time to get married, or the right time to go back to school.

Let the inner witness guide you in all things. This is one of my absolute greatest findings. God doesn't just care about your church, business or your ministry. He wants you to live a successful, abundant, having plenty, more than adequate, over-sufficient life (John 10:10 AMP)! John 14:26 AMP reminds us that the *Helper (Comforter, Advocate, Intercessor—Counselor, Strengthener, Standby), the Holy Spirit, whom the Father will send in My name [in My place, to represent Me and act on My behalf], He will teach you all things*. He is concerned about all things *YOU*!

I know you thought I forgot about the red light. And I did lol! I got so caught up sharing about God's timing. Anywho, the red light actually brings me to another way I believe God speaks. I like to call them Divine halts. God will often give you a feeling of unrest: a halt, a "hold up," a , "Whoa there!"

My former Pastor used to say that God orders both our steps and our stops, (Psalms 119:133). Isn't that good?! Has the Spirit ever stopped you from doing something, going somewhere or saying something? I can literally attest to the fact that He has. I appreciate the Holy Spirit because He has stopped me from doing some of the crazy things I think sometimes. I am a lot more bold than what He will sometimes allow me to prove. There are moments I wish the Lord would let me say or post certain things but He just won't. And even when I do it anyway, I have to delete it. Some of y'all know what I'm talking about. How many times do we override divine halts? Again, I can testify that there have been sooooooo many times that I ignored the halt of God. I wanna tell you about two.

The other day, I was in the airport coming back from an amazing trip to the Dominican Republic. My mom and sister and I were in the airport. Given the fact that we had to be there at least three hours early, we decided to try and finish a game of Phase Ten from the night before. Of course I'm talking trash and enjoying the game. If you know anything about Phase Ten, you must always pick up a card and put down a card. If anyone has already put down a card that you have, you want to keep it in your hand or get rid of it so that they cannot pick up the card that has already been phased out (If you don't understand sorry. Feel free to pick up a deck of PT cards. It's quite a fun game). Long story less long, there were exactly three times in the game that I felt a halt. Seriously like an, "Aht aht, don't put that card down."

I kid you not, every time I felt it, I ignored it, put down the card, and my sister used it against us. She actually won the game because I just didn't listen. To be honest, I hope to get so good at hearing God, that no one wants to play with me because I always win. Not sure if God cares who wins the next game of Charades or Texas Hold 'em, but it doesn't hurt to try. On a more serious note, there was an incident that happened that I will not soon forget. I've not even told three people the background behind this story until now. Well before I became a full-time entrepreneur, I was a supervisor in the sales field. I loved my job until I didn't, (but that's a different story). The position afforded me the opportunity to meet and interact with all kinds of people. Because I'm so introverted, it made it a little easier to build relationships.

I remember meeting a lady on the job and because she liked to cook, sing and laugh we instantly connected. However, I vividly remember the halts that the Holy Spirit had given me. My thought was oh she loves Gospel music, goes to church, makes everybody laugh, a gym partner, surely there is no harm. Of course, I totally ignored it even after it had been confirmed that it probably wasn't a good idea to associate myself with her. I quickly realized why I had felt the halt in my spirit. Drama seemed to follow her wherever she went, but by that time was it too late? Some time ago I was leaving work early in the morning and was in an accident that *totaled* the car. Did you hear what I said!? I said the accident took my car but was unauthorized to take my life! I almost got happy and threw this laptop! *Calms self...woosah*

It was my first real accident and it startled me to say the least. What you don't know is that at the very moment and I mean, the very moment, I was hit by a drunk driver, I was texting the very person my mind, people and the Holy Spirit told me to run from. Yes, I was texting and driving so much so that I didn't know if the accident was my fault or not until I saw that I was hit from behind. I don't know about you, but I know without a shadow of a doubt that this was not a coincidence. God used that accident to literally wake me up and open my eyes to several things in my life that I was oblivious to. You need some Bible? I got you. Acts 16:6 (Voice), *"They sensed the Holy Spirit telling them not to preach their message in Asia at this time, so they traveled through Phrygia and Galatia."* Here we have Paul and his compadres going out to preach the Gospel, but the Holy Spirit told them not to go to Asia. While the scripture doesn't say why, I don't think it matters. If the Holy Spirit knows everything (and He does), we must trust the fact that both He does and that He has our best interest at heart. The Holy Spirit is the helper, so let Him help you (John 14:26).

I need you to understand why I used these examples. The first is to show you that God really is concerned with everything about you. Again, maybe not every game you play, but certainly every move you make. The second to show you something God said to me even several months after my accident. He said, "If I can't get in your ear, I'll get in your life." Take a moment and let that sink in. *iListened*. God wants to speak to you and often goes to great lengths to be heard. John, the apostle, was on the beach near Patmos, heard a voice like a trumpet telling him to be a scribe for what he was about to see (John 1). He took Moses to the back of the desert and spoke through a bush that was on fire, but wouldn't burn up (Exodus). He had Saul, who was soon to be Paul, on the road to Damascus. Shone a bright light from Heaven, threw him off his animal, and blinded him (Acts 9).

What could you be experiencing as a direct result of the fact that God is trying to get your attention? What does He want to say to you that you're missing out on? Here's the grace of God. All things work together for good (Romans 8:28). And I love the way the Amplified version says it. *"And we know [with great confidence] that God [who is deeply concerned about us] causes all things to work together [as a plan] for good for those who love God, to those who are called according to His purpose."* I was able to use the time from my accident to refocus both emotionally, spiritually and financially. It was the push I needed to become a full-time entrepreneur as He was also leading me to do. It was me taking *my* sweet time. The grace is in the fact that God uses even your willful ignorance, to ignite the flames of passion for what He has called you to do. Isn't that amazing?! My accident is the perfect example of Romans 8:28. All things were and still are working for good.

God Speaks Through People

I told you about a situation I had to deal with publicly, but I didn't really give detail on how it changed me on the inside. I started directing, singing and playing at a young age. This caused me to have to lead and often be out front. When this is the case, people often see the effect of the anointing on your life, sometimes without even knowing it. My personality with a mic, and without one, were totally different. I have always appeared to be an outgoing person, but inwardly extremely introverted. As I got older and deal with public scrutiny, it caused me to really draw back from everyone and to create my own little bubble to live in. I still served in ministry, but I would literally walk straight out the door as soon as the benediction was given.

If I didn't see you on the way to my car, you would just have to call because I was ghost, (gone in the wind, for the non-millenials that may read this lol). I allowed the violent storms of life, some self-inflicted and some just by happenstance, to strip me of the God-given voice I had once used so passionately. Not just my singing voice, but the voice God had given me to herald the importance of a relationship with Him. Here I was this multi-gifted mute, who was determined not to need anyone, especially, "church people." After all, they were the ones I trusted to help, encourage and strengthen me, yet they were the very ones that broke my heart. It caused me to trust *no* one.

One of the most hurtful things is to love people who you can no longer trust. To be completely honest, I am still working through issues, but what I came to realize is that you need people. In fact, how can you truly trust God and not trust people? Not in a sense that you go around naive, but in a sense of, "Even if someone does hurt me, I trust God to heal me and even use the pain for my good." I can say with certainty that everyone who will read this book has been hurt, but the testimony is that you're still alive. The hurt may have harmed you, but the sting didn't kill you. I said all that to say…You need people. Point blank. Period. The, "Long as I got King Jesus..." mentality is in fact, not Biblical or Christ-like at all, (sorry Vickie). The beauty of the Kingdom of God, or body of Christ, is that it's not just one person or a group of people who are all alike. The beauty of the Kingdom is our differences; our strengths and weaknesses. Look at the principles and Scriptures that show us why we need each other.

1. We become together what we could not be alone.

Romans 12:4-6 (MSG) In this way we are like the various parts of a human body. Each part gets its meaning from the body as a whole, not the other way around. The body we're talking about is Christ's body of chosen people. Each of us finds our meaning and function as a part of his body. But as a chopped-off finger or cut-off toe we wouldn't amount to much, would we? So since we find ourselves fashioned into all these excellently formed and marvelously functioning parts in Christ's body, let's just go ahead and be what we were made to be, without enviously or pridefully comparing ourselves with each other, or trying to be something we aren't.

2. Real friends make you better, and provide accountability.

Proverbs 27:17 *(Voice) In the same way that iron sharpens iron, a person sharpens the character of his friend.*

3. Burdens become *less heavy when (and only when) you learn to share them.*

Galatians 6:2 (AMP) Carry one another's burdens and in this way you will fulfill the requirements of the law of Christ [that is, the law of Christian love].

4. Restoration is the responsibility of the spiritually mature, realizing that it's them today, but could be you tonight.

Galatians 6:1 (NLT) *Dear brothers and sisters, if another believer is overcome by some sin, you who are godly should gently and humbly help that person back onto the right path. And be careful not to fall into the same temptation yourself.*

Had to give you some Bible. I often say that, "It may be easy to argue with me, but it's hard arguing with the Word of God." Now, I know, people can be a lot to deal with, especially if you are an introvert, like me. I mean I'm walk-all-they-way-down-another-grocery-aisle-just-to-avoid-the-uncomfortability-of-speaking-to-someone bad - no exaggeration. If I could be successful and be what God called me to be and not have to deal with people, I would JUMP at the chance. But here's the thing, God didn't gift you for you. He gifted you to share your gift with the world. And if no one has told you already, YOU are a gift! You're not just gifted. You are a gift!

You may be thinking, "Why are we talking about this? What does it have to do with hearing God's voice?" Well it is important to understand how precious you are. It is important to understand just how much God values your imperfect self. So much so that He wants, not only to speak to you, but speak through you. He will not just speak to you about you, but will speak to you for and about others. Don't you want to be God's messenger? To operate in the spiritual gifts of the word of knowledge or prophecy? How awesome is it to be able to articulate what God is saying? I think it is absolutely incredible and hope that you are beginning to as well!

God uses people to prophesy and to confirm what He has already spoken to you. Have you ever heard God, and wondered if it was your thought or Him speaking only for someone else to come and say the same thing? I have. It is one of the dopest things to me. Sometimes we hear God speaking and either don't want to hear what we heard or genuinely don't realize that it was Him at all. I was taught in seminary that any time God says something more than once you had better pay attention and not ignore its importance. It makes me think of the story of Samuel.

1 Samuel 3:3-10 (NIV)

3 The lamp of God had not yet gone out, and Samuel was lying down in the house of the Lord, where the ark of God was. 4 Then the Lord called Samuel.

Samuel answered, "Here I am." 5 And he ran to Eli and said, "Here I am; you called me." But Eli said, "I did not call; go back and lie down." So he went and lay down.

6 Again the Lord called, "Samuel!" And Samuel got up and went to Eli and said, "Here I am; you called me." "My son," Eli said, "I did not call; go back and lie down." 7 Now Samuel did not yet know the Lord: The word of the Lord had not yet been revealed to him. 8 A third time the Lord called, "Samuel!" And Samuel got up and went to Eli and said, "Here I am; you called me." Then Eli realized that the Lord was calling the boy.

9 So Eli told Samuel, "Go and lie down, and if he calls you, say, 'Speak, Lord, for your servant is listening.'" So Samuel went and lay down in his place.

10 The Lord came and stood there, calling as at the other times, "Samuel! Samuel!"

Then Samuel said, "Speak, for your servant is listening."

There are two things I want to point out from this story. When God spoke to Samuel, but he was not able to recognize the Voice, Eli was there to help. Another reason why we need people, is because we need mentors. Samuel is new to hearing God's voice, but he has a priest and mentor who had the ability to know when God was speaking to Him. You should seek mentors. There must be people in your life who can hear God when you can't. There must be people in your life who have been where you are trying to go and can, with God's help, walk you there. This goes back to those of us who think we can do everything on our own, but one thing is for certain. God uses people to speak and confirm what He has said.

The second thing I think is important to share with you is the flip side of needing people. Understand that people are just that. People. None of us are perfect. None of us know it all. That is the importance of a balance of needing people yet totally trusting in God. While Eli was able to help Samuel, how many of us are like Samuel? How many of us run to other people to validate what they never said in the first place? I have learned in this journey of hearing God that He is your most reliable source. It goes back to the importance of a relationship with Him and knowing His Word. I'll be completely honest with you. Sometimes people think they heard God when they really haven't. Maybe it was something in their subconscious thoughts and or feelings. Maybe something they ate and sometimes maybe even a result of something they heard or think they saw. **Psalm 119:105** (MSG) says, "...*it is by your words I can see where I'm going; they throw a beam of light on my dark path.* For the Word of God is living and active *and* full of power [making it operative, energizing, and effective]. It is sharper than any two-edged sword, penetrating as far as the division of the soul and spirit [the completeness of a person], and of both joints and marrow [the deepest parts of our nature], exposing *and* judging the very thoughts and intentions of the heart (**Hebrews 4:12** AMP)." What am I saying? Let prayer and God's Word be the point of reference by which every other word is judged and then obey His instruction. I have personally come to the conclusion at this point in my life that If I feel God is saying something, I would rather be wrong than disobedient.

Chapter 3
When God Speaks

Matthew 4:4 KJV, *"But he answered and said, It is written, Man shall not live by bread alone, but by every word that **proceedeth** out of the mouth of God."* For most of the book, I have avoided the King James version simply because it can sometimes be difficult to understand. I thought it necessary, however, to look at this particular Scripture in this translation for the purposes of breaking down a few things. Yes, I am about to have a slight seminarian moment, but it will support my point. I promise to keep it short, sweet and to the point.

The New Testament was written in Greek. I thought it imperative to look at the meaning of this Scripture in its original language to fully understand the meaning. To understand the meaning of words you must look at the mood, voice and tense of the word. For example, the mood of "proceedeth" is participle. According to BlueLetterBible.com, the Greek participle corresponds for the most part to the English participle, reflecting "**-ing**" or "-ed" being suffixed to the basic verb form. The voice of the word, "proceedeth," is what is called middle or passive deponent. This means that in almost all cases, the word is translated as being in the **active voice**. And lastly, the present tense represents a simple statement of fact or reality viewed as, **occurring in actual time**. If that isn't enough the English definition of proceedeth, or proceeds, is to begin or continue a course of action. I believe Jesus was saying that we are sustained not just by what God has said, but by what God is saying and what He will say. In other words, God is *always* speaking.

I recently read an article about how radio stations work. I look at it this way. There are radio stations in every state and city in America. With the number of radio stations available, many, if not most, cities that may not even have a station, still have broadcasting coverage. Your radio is a way of sending energy with waves. "In other words, it's a method of transmitting electrical energy from one place to another without using any kind of direct, wired connection."

An AM station will broadcast a signal at a constant frequency, but is only amplified when the constant signals are met by sound signals. It is the tuner that causes the radio to find the desired frequency and ignore everything else in the air. Now, you may not understand the science of it all, but know this, as long as you are listening on the right frequency, you will always have access to what is being broadcasted. What God wants to say to you is He's always accessible. Stop tuning Him out and learn to tune in what He is speaking.

Tuning in often means silencing all other frequencies. Many times, the frequency of television is too loud. Other times, the frequency of social media consumes our ears and mind. Other times, it may be the voices of others that are drowning out the voice of the Holy Spirit. Whatever may be the cause of the muted Voice, it is up to you to realize that when all is said and done, God knows best. I need YOU to be the one to provide spiritual coverage to those around you who are disconnected from the only source of life, Jesus Christ! Live every day with the eager expectation that any moment He may say something that will alter the course of your entire life and anyone connected to you.

I'd even take it a step further and say that we, as the body of Christ, should never be caught off guard. Not about anything, from the latest news stories to even our death. I strongly believe that if there is anything we don't know, someone wasn't listening. Now I know I probably ruffled some religious feathers with these statements, but hear me out. First, the Word of God tells us in **Amos 3:7** that God does absolutely *nothing* without first revealing it to His messengers. But why did 9/11 shock everyone? Did someone miss the word of the Lord? But why did Columbine come as a surprise? What about the devastation of Hurricane Katrina? Where were the prophets? Where are the people who even want to hear God?!

Now I know some of you may disagree, but hear me out. While you may never agree, one of my goals is to be an initiator of thought. Think about the story of Noah and the ark (**Genesis 6:9-9:17**). God clearly spoke to Noah not only that an incredible flood was coming, but how to navigate through what was coming. Noah was given specific instructions from the type of wood to use and even the exact measurements of each material that was to be used to build the ark. Noah not only obeyed God's instructions on how to construct that ark, but He also warned the people that a flood like never before was to wipe out the earth. This story is important because it shows someone who has clearly heard from God, but people who rejected what they heard.

I believe that sometimes it is not that God didn't speak nor that His prophets and prophetic people did not speak, but that it is us, the hearers, who sometimes do not heed the word of God. The story of Noah is a prime example. This was not a matter of Noah not hearing God. It was a matter of people not listening to His servant. How many warnings do you think you have missed out on, not because someone didn't hear God, but because you disregarded what God was trying to say? Many times we walk in an often untouched sin called pride. Some of us simply think we know everything or that we have the power to control what only God can control. **Proverbs 16:18** (Voice) reminds us that *pride precedes destruction; an arrogant spirit gives way to a nasty fall.*

Someone maybe asking how could it be possible to know or be warned about disasters and catastrophes that may happen? The same way Samuel warned King Saul. The same way Noah warned the people of the day that a flood was coming. The same way John the Baptist told us to repent for the Kingdom of Heaven is at hand and to prepare the way of the Lord. Well maybe that's not enough and you're wondering if God really speaks concerning death. In fact, several people who walked closely with God knew when their time was ending. Jacob knew. Joseph knew. Paul knew. I even believed that Abraham knew. They all were able to bless their children before death and in death. They all had the ability to get their business straight and prepare generation that would come behind them.

A lot of people don't want to think about death, but personally, I would want to know when my time is coming to an end. We as millennials, often live as if we have forever, but forever is not promised to us on Earth. I want to be able to share Paul's sentiments from **2 Timothy 4:6-7** (KJV).

> *"For I am now ready to be offered, and the time of my departure is at hand. I have fought a good fight, I have finished **my** course, I have kept the faith. "*

When it's all said and done, I want it to be said that I did everything I was supposed to do. We have to always be sure to care enough for our families and ministry to the point that we even seek God's direction on who to pass the baton to, whether in life or death. Someone has got to be listening. Will it be you?

Believe it or not, sometimes I hear people's objections as I'm talking. As I was writing, I heard the objection, "If God speaks everything to us, what about the scripture that says that we know and prophesy in part?" Well I'm glad you asked. **1 Corinthians 13:9** (AMP) says that we know in part, and we prophesy in part [for our knowledge is fragmentary and incomplete]. The Amplified version, in my opinion can sometimes be a little wordy, but I love the way it communicates this scripture. It is true. Our knowledge is limited, but the Holy Spirit's knowledge is never ending. If the Holy Spirit will teach us in all things, then He must know all things.

Secondly, I do also believe that God does not give us every single detail of every single thing, but I look at it like this. What if my friend calls and tells me that a burglar is on the way to my house? *I* have a choice whether to *listen* or not. I may not know the specific identity of the person. I may not know what color their eyes are. I may not know how old he or she is. I may not even know their name. I know in part, but that does not negate the fact that I have a sense of what will happen. It also does not negate the fact that I must adequately prepare and summon a power Higher than me to stop what I know is coming. The same is true for what God may show you or how He may warn you. Although you may not know all the details, mercy has thrown you a lifeline. Listen to what the Holy Spirit is saying to you.

Yes, God is always speaking. I believe however, that He stops the ears of those who will not hearken to His voice. Have you ever been in a situation with someone where you kept saying that same thing to them over and over and over again? How does that make you feel? For me, it's super frustrating. It makes you wonder why am I wasting my breath and thoughts on someone who is not even listening? I remember when I was in my teenage years. I was much younger, but still old enough to make my own decisions. My parents would tell me what to do and of course I would question it. For most things, they would just give me that, "Okay, you're grown." After a while, they just stopped talking about certain things. But when things went terribly wrong, I remembered the instructions they gave that I just ignored. As I got older, I realized that what I felt was keeping me from what I wanted to do was keeping me out of the hand and harm of the enemy. What should have followed their words of wisdom was my obedience.

We have talked a lot about why God speaks. We've talked about several of the ways God speaks. We've talked about when God speaks. However, please understand before we move any further that the only response to God's voice is obedience. I can't stress that enough. The prophet Samuel reminds us that obedience is far better than sacrifice (**1Samuel 15:22**). This was the response to King

Saul that had once again disobeyed God's instructions. Saul takes the animals of his enemies that God told him to destroy. Instead, he takes them for himself. On top of that, he offers some of the animals as sacrifices to God in worship. How many of us offer up to God the product of our disobedience as if we're right? You offer up a tip when He told you to tithe. He told you to follow peace with all men, but instead you offer to Him the ugly excuse of *in my best ratchet voice* "this is just how I am." You brag of your knowledge of the only scripture you know verbatim, "Jesus wept" meanwhile you know every Beyonce album from Destiny's Child to Homecoming. He said to hide His Word in your heart so that you have a better chance of overcoming sin. Jesus said if you love me obey my commands (**John 14:15**).

Obedience is key. Obedience even more trumps your worship. God tells Saul to destroy the Amalekites and everything that belongs to them. Saul keeps the best of the sheep and cattle to offer it to God in worship. It is then that the prophet Samuel reminds Saul that obedience is the principal thing (**1 Samuel 15:22**). In fact, if devotion is the key that unlocks the door of the supernatural, obedience is the door stopper that keeps the door open. I don't know about you, but I need the supernatural door of favor and power to stay open 24/7 for me!

Many in the Bible were totally dependent on God's instructions. It was the only way to be successful. Take Abraham for example. God tells him to leave his family and go to a place He'd show him. Now if it were me, I'd be like, "Now God you gone have to give me more than that. I need to know where I'm going so I can put it in my GPS." But here is Abraham, the father of faith, going to a place that was unknown to him, only to receive more instructions. I believe for many of us, that we are not clear on what to do next because we have yet to be obedient to His last instruction. I challenge you to go back and do what He *said* so that you can hear what He wants to say. Watch how obedience to the last instruction will put a demand on Heaven to release the next one.

There is one other ingredient that is necessary in hearing God. I believe you must check your heart regularly. **Jeremiah 17:9** says that, *"The heart is deceitful above all things, and desperately wicked: who can know it?"* God certainly does. I know you probably think your heart is Mr. Clean clean, but the Bible explicitly tells us that, unfortunately, it isn't. Because our hearts are naturally wicked, we've got to check our motives and intentions often. In other words, you *must* have integrity! Prophetic people don't have the right to be "petty." In fact, there are few things more dangerous than anointed people who lack honesty and honor. Prophetic people who lack integrity are the equivalent of a toddler with a gun in their hand; death or destruction is soon to follow. Prophetic people don't lie on their taxes. Prophetic people don't use FMLA to go to that mall. Prophetic people don't let their kids tell the bill collector that, "My mama said she not here." Prophetic people have leaders in their local assembly...that they submit to. I don't care what example you had, we must not become products the negativity we have seen, but rather trailblazers in what God wants to do.

There are some things that should not be named among us. That's old school for, "where they do that at?" We must be vessels of purity and honor. I don't want to have to go on a 40-day fast and stop watching shows I shouldn't be watching in the first place for God to be able to use me. There's an old song I used to hear as a little girl that I try my best to live by. It says "I want to live so God can use me, anywhere Lord, anytime." I pray that this is your daily prayer. After all, our foundational text in **1 Corinthians 14:1** shows us that before we desire the gifts of the Spirit, we must aggressively pursue love. And if you go back one chapter to 1 Corinthians 13, you will find that Paul tells you exactly what love is and is not, what love does and does not do.

1 Corinthians 13:1-8 (AMP)

1 If I speak with the tongues of men and of angels, but have not [a]love [for others growing out of God's love for me], then I have become only a noisy gong or a clanging cymbal [just an annoying distraction]. 2 And if I have the gift of prophecy [and speak a new message from God to the people], and understand all mysteries, and [possess] all knowledge; and if I have all [sufficient] faith so that I can remove mountains, but do not have love [reaching out to others], I am nothing. **3** If I give all my possessions to feed the poor, and if I surrender my body [b]to be burned, but do not have love, it does me no good at all. **4** Love endures with patience and serenity, love is kind and thoughtful, and is not jealous or envious; love does not brag and is not proud or arrogant. **5** It is not rude; it is not self-seeking, it is not provoked [nor overly sensitive and easily angered]; it does not take into account a wrong endured. **6** It does not rejoice at injustice, but rejoices with the truth [when right and truth prevail]. **7** Love bears all things [regardless of what comes], believes all things [looking for the best in each one], hopes all things [remaining steadfast during difficult times], endures all things [without weakening]. **8** Love never fails [it never fades nor ends]. But as for prophecies, they will pass away; as for tongues, they will cease; as for the gift of special knowledge, it will pass away.

This excerpt is sooooo loaded. I could probably write a whole 'notha book on this chapter alone. However, I want to bring up that this Scripture says that you if don't love, keep your prophecy. Paul literally says you can speak several languages including your Heavenly language, but at the end of the day it still means nothing. All your gifts will pass away except for the love you have for God's people. It's important that you understand this because God will sometimes give you confidential information about people. I believe that God only speaks sensitive information to the purest of hearts. You have a responsibility to consider their business as you would want yours considered. You have a responsibility to go before God not to gossip. You have a charge to live with love and integrity.

Chapter 4
What God Speaks

Ok let's take a moment to review what we've discussed thus far. God speaks because He loves you, cares about you and wants the best for you. God is always speaking. It is when we obey what He has already said that He gives the next steps. God speaks through the spirit of God that was in the earth since the before time existed. Through consistent devotion, our spirit echoes what the Holy Spirit is saying. God speaks through His Word. God speaks through people. God speaks to you from within. God speaks through pictures and series of pictures both when we are asleep and when we are awake. Now let's take a deeper look at what God speaks.

God speaks what He wants to speak. He is sovereign. To be sovereign literally means to possess supreme power which further means that He can do whatever He wants. I'm so glad He's not only a sovereign King, but a loving Father. What good Father sees their child in need and doesn't help? God is concerned about you and will speak wisdom, warnings, destiny and direction.

Wisdom

What is Godly wisdom? This is something that has honestly frustrated me for years. The Bible says that the fear of the Lord is the beginning of wisdom, (**Proverbs 1:7**). Not fear in the sense of being scared, but to respect, regard and reverence. Ok, got it. That's the beginning, but what *is* wisdom? I have heard others say that wisdom is experience, but I don't think that is the full extent of wisdom. Solomon's one request to God was for wisdom, specifically to lead the people. However, if that is the case, and wisdom is experience, that piece of the puzzle would not properly fit because Solomon had no former experience with being a king. There is not an explicit definition in the Word of God (at least not that I have found), but I believe wisdom is the God-given ability to lead, act, and judge based on experience(s) and knowledge for which you do not have. One of the greatest examples of wisdom was this story of how Solomon judges these two characters.

1 Kings 3:16- 28

16 Some time later two prostitutes came to the king to have an argument settled.17 "Please, my lord," one of them began, "this woman and I live in the same house. I gave birth to a baby while she was with me in the house. 18

Three days later this woman also had a baby. We were alone; there were only two of us in the house. **19** *"But her baby died during the night when she rolled over on it.* **20** *Then she got up in the night and took my son from beside me while I was asleep. She laid her dead child in my arms and took mine to sleep beside her.* **21** *And in the morning when I tried to nurse my son, he was dead! But when I looked more closely in the morning light, I saw that it wasn't my son at all."* **22** *Then the other woman interrupted, "It certainly was your son, and the living child is mine." "No," the first woman said, "the living child is mine, and the dead one is yours." And so they argued back and forth before the king.* **23** *Then the king said, "Let's get the facts straight. Both of you claim the living child is yours, and each says that the dead one belongs to the other.* **24** *All right, bring me a sword." So a sword was brought to the king.* **25** *Then he said, "Cut the living child in two, and give half to one woman and half to the other!"* **26** *Then the woman who was the real mother of the living child, and who loved him very much, cried out, "Oh no, my lord! Give her the child—please do not kill him!" But the other woman said, "All right, he will be neither yours nor mine; divide him between us!"* **27** *Then the king said, "Do not kill the child, but give him to the woman who wants him to live, for she is his mother!"* **28** *When all Israel heard the king's decision, the people were in awe of the king, for they saw the wisdom God had given him for rendering justice.*

God speaks through His wisdom so that we may have

Divine understanding. I have experienced the wisdom of God through a dream. I dreamt that someone very close to me had attempted suicide not once, but twice. Not only did the dream help me to understand something that I had already been feeling, but also gave me the wisdom on how to handle this person moving forward. This is so important when hearing God about other people, because you never know what people are going through, but He is, "the only wise God." Rarely does wisdom just fall in your lap. It must be pursued and sought as a glorious treasure. **Proverbs 3:13-18** encourages us that *"You're blessed when you meet Lady Wisdom, when you make friends with Madame Insight. She's worth far more than money in the bank; her friendship is better than a big salary. Her value exceeds all the trappings of wealth;nothing you could wish for holds a candle to her. With one hand she gives long life, with the other she confers recognition. Her manner is beautiful, her life wonderfully complete. She's the very Tree of Life to those who embrace her. Hold her tight—and be blessed!"*

Warnings

Checed (pronounced kheh'-sed) is the Hebrew word for mercy. This describes the amazing kindness and pity that God has on you and me. To think about the fact that His mercy endures forever is such a mind-blowing concept. Mercy is not a cup that ever runs dry. I wouldn't encourage it, but you cannot even out sin God's mercy. What it means is that I don't care how much you or I miss the mark, there will still be mercy generations to come. Hallelujah! It is the beautiful mercy of God that sends warnings to us. The Scriptures are loaded with warnings, whether straight from the mouth of God, His prophets, apostles, or even just a vessel willing to speak truth. Paul warned us in **2 Thessalonians 2:3** that the Antichrist would come and not to be deceived by the self-exalted one. Moses warned Pharaoh to let His people be free to worship or calamity would come, (Exodus 5). And God, Himself, warns us more often than most of us realize.

For example, I was in the mountains with my family and had a dream that we were going on an excursion. My mother was near a body of water. I tried to go with her because even in the dream, I was concerned and I was not allowed to accompany her. I woke up very concerned and troubled in my spirit. All I could do was bind death, disease and disaster. I went into the room, got some oil and prayed for her. At first, she thought I was being a clown as usual so she had a play play baptist fit. (We clown around quite often and no offense to my Baptist-born, Baptist-bred...saints) Once she realized that I was serious, she received what I was saying, as she knows I don't play about what God shows me. Needless to say, we stayed far away from water the rest of the trip. I don't know what God shielded her from that weekend but it certainly was not worth the risk. Thank God for warnings!

Purpose and Destiny

When I was a young girl, I had a terrifying dream. I will never forget it for as long as I live. It wasn't a dream of me falling, (although I have some of those). It wasn't a dream of the "boogie man." It wasn't even about monsters under my bed. I had a dream that I was ministering to a crowd so big, I couldn't see the end of it. At the time, I didn't know whether I was singing or teaching or what I was doing. As I got older, I felt that I was preaching and or prophesying, which of course increased the anxiety and fear. I was an adult before I ever told anyone about this purpose/destiny dream. God was showing me at an early age what the course of my life would look like. God has a way of showing you the end from the beginning, whether in a dream, prophecy, an inner knowing or otherwise (**Isaiah 46:10**). I wish I hadn't kept this to myself for so long. Sometimes, I wonder if I would have been "further along" had I let someone in and allowed them to mentor me, instead of hiding in fear. Nonetheless, I am thankful that I know what I know about my purpose and destiny.

This brings to my mind one of my favorite Bible stories. The story of Joseph. At a young age, Joseph was given a dream that would illuminate the destiny God had for him. Take a quick look at **Genesis 37:5-11**. *One day Joseph had a dream. When he told the dream to his brothers, they hated him even more.* **Joseph: 6** *Please listen to this dream I had!* **7** *There we were, binding sheaves in the field. Suddenly, my sheaf rose and stood up, and then* your sheaves all gathered around it and bowed down to my sheaf. **Joseph's Brothers** (annoyed): **8** Are you serious? You think you are somehow destined to reign over us? You think you are going to be our king? This dream and what he told them about it made them hate him even more. **9** But Joseph had another dream, and he made the mistake of telling them about this dream too. **Joseph:** Listen! I've had another dream: I saw the sun, the moon, and 11 stars bowing down to me. **10** When he told this dream to his father and brothers, even his father scolded him. **Israel:** What kind of dream is this? Do you actually think your mother and I and your brothers are going to bow down before you? **11** Joseph's brothers had become extremely jealous of him. But his father—though he scolded Joseph—kept this dream in the back of his mind.

Joseph had a destiny dream at a very young age. Not everyone is fortunate enough to know what their life will look like so early in life. It can be one of the most frustrating things in life to be ignorant of your purpose; the reason why God placed you on the earth. While purpose and destiny work together, I think it is important to understand the distinct difference between the two. Purpose is your reason for existence, while destiny is the target for where your life is headed. Both purpose and destiny were predetermined by God, however destiny can be altered while purpose can not. ☐ Destiny can be altered simply because destiny (destination) is a product of the choices we make. God may have a predestined (destiny) plan, however it takes knowing the steps between purpose and destiny to able to attain it. In order to avoid living aimlessly you too must pursue purpose and destiny. Your life and someone else's life depends on it.

Direction/Instruction

Many times in life, we are one instruction away from where God wants us to be. He gives instructions to help us along the path of righteousness and abundant living. Instructions not only affect us, but they also affect those closest to us. Unfollowed instructions even affect those that God has called us to, that we may not even know yet. We absolutely need instructions and direction. Many people make visions and plans for themselves that God never intended. It is important to acknowledge Him in *all* our ways so that He can direct our steps. I often hear people quote **Habakkuk 2:2** that says, "Write the vision, make it plain," as if to say that you must write your vision and make it plain. While I agree that you should write out a vision for your life, family and ministry, it takes looking at the context of the Scripture to understand what is actually happening. The entire book of Habakkuk is literally a conversation between the prophet and God. I challenge you to go read the book and see for yourself. It's only three chapters.

Sidenote: Habakkuk is quite a mouthful to pronounce so for the purposes of ease, I'm giving him a nickname. Hab goes to God and asked him several questions about why the people are having to suffer at the hands of their enemies. Go after the answers the first set of questions comes back and says write the vision and make it plain, so that others can read it. It may take some time, but you will soon understand what I'm about to tell you. So if it doesn't come as soon as you think, just wait for it. In other words, God was not telling him to write down his vision, but rather His answer, revelation, vision, what God was about to show him. God was telling him to write down what I show you. I believe we should take that principle and apply it to our lives. Take what God is speaking and showing you and let that be the basis for your destiny plans, not your desires, not what others think you should, but His plan, His vision, His instructions. As Christians, we will continue to live below are means if we do not take full advantage of the opportunities God's direction affords us. Follow the Voice and it will *never* lead you wrong!

Conclusion

I really, really hope and pray that your hunger has been stirred for the presence of God. You may say wait I thought this book was about God's voice. Have you ever been in someone's presence who is known to talk a lot and they say nothing? Probably not. If you can just get in His presence He *will* speak. Know that God's presence is better than money. If you can just make being in His presence a daily experience, it will change your life. It will heal your heart. It will calm your temper. God's presence can do what no one else's can. I hope that you have read this book and want to know what *your* spiritual gifts are and seek to know more about how to fully operate in them.

I can't stress enough the importance of appreciating your own journey. Yours is almost certain not to look like anyone else's and that is okay! God deals with me in dreams, but He may deal with you in an open vision. You may not sound like, "everyone else." Maybe your gift won't manifest right away. Take your time and be consistent. I was on the highway one day. I was speeding as I sometimes do. I passed a car and happened to look over at the driver. I'm not sure, but maybe he thought we were in a scene of, "Fast and Furious." As I looked in my rearview mirror, I saw him quickly approaching. In my mind, I'm wondering, "Where did he come from?" The next thing I knew he was on my tail so I pulled over in the middle lane to let him pass. He passed me and looked over as if to say "now who's in the lead?" I chuckled because in my mind I was thinking, "You idiot, I wasn't even thinking about you." It was in that moment that I heard God say something that I often say to myself, when the spirit of comparison is rising up. "Always be in a hurry, but never in a race." Be diligent in doing what you have been called to do and leave the competition in the stadiums and arenas. We've wasted enough time and have no more to waste. We must be about our Father's business. If we are doing that to the extent that we should, there's no time left for competition. Focus on completing not competing and I believe God will honor that.

To the person that feels like they're just not ready to give God everything, to the person who is like I am, "Tired of [this] church," to anyone who will read this who loves God, but maybe not the representation of His church that you've experienced, to the person who is in church physically every time the doors are open, but absent in mind and spirit, listen closely to what I'm about to say. God loves you so much! And so do I! I have such a heart for people like you because I was you. Yep, church *all* my life, but completely and utterly over it all. I understand that you may feel like church may not be for you. I understand you want to get your life right before you get saved. I understand, "church people" may have hurt you.

I understand it may feel like this Christianity thing is only about rules; what I can and can't wear, what I can and can't say. I get it. And on behalf of the church, I would like to apologize to you. I apologize for those who made you feel like you had to have everything right in order to come to church and God. It should be the same thing. I apologize on behalf of the judgmental religious people who made you feel like, "saved people," wear this or wear that. I'm sorry that they weren't spiritual enough to see your inside from looking at your image; the ones that cared more about keeping you under their control more than your condition. I apologize to the ones who grew up in church and were disgusted by the double standards, guilty gossipers and abusive leaders.

I apologize to every PK (preacher's kid) that saw their parents abused in the name of Jesus. Every PK whose parents didn't know a healthy balance between their family and the church family; whose games, recitals and big moments were eclipsed by revivals, services and member visitations. I hope you will understand that church people are still people. They make mistakes just like everyone else. That does not give them an excuse or pass, but it does put things in perspective. A part of our issue is our small view of God. We often put pastors and leaders on a pedestal only God should occupy, making it difficult to truly see Him. In some cases, it is not until Uzziah dies that we see the Lord (Isaiah 6). I am not saying that our leaders must die but I am saying that we've got to change our perspective. We must see God so big that it's hard to pay attention to anything else because He has your undivided attention. I challenge you to what James talks about in **James 4:8-10** (MSG). *So let God work his will in you. Yell a loud no to the Devil and watch him scamper. Say a quiet yes to God and he'll be there in no time. Quit dabbling in sin. Purify your inner life. Quit playing the field. Hit bottom, and cry your eyes out. Get serious, really serious. Get down on your knees before the Master; it's the only way you'll get on your feet.* God wants to speak to you. Listen.

I pray that every leader reading this will not just say oh this was a good read, but that they will share it with their circle of influence. I say this with the utmost respect. If our churches are not aware, nor open to the fact, that young adults have spiritual gifts, the generations behind us are in trouble; the church is in trouble. There is a major problem if we are not training our youth and young adults in the gifts of the spirit and five-fold administration, (apostles, prophets, evangelists, pastors, teachers). If in fact, each of these are not in operation, we are failing to adequately mature God's people, to effectively work in ministry and build up the body of Christ. You may have thought how dare you or how could you say such a thing with such confidence? Easy. **Ephesians 4:11-12** (NKJV) *And He Himself gave some to be apostles, some prophets, some evangelists, and some pastors and teachers, for the equipping of the saints for the work of ministry, for the edifying of the body of Christ.*

I've been a victim of being confined to where there was a need even if it wasn't where I need to be. Our bands and worship teams ought to know what their gifts are and be *trained* in them. Our praise dance teams ought to know what their gifts are and be *trained* in them. Our media teams ought to know what their gifts are and be *trained* in them. I may be biased to only mention the arts, but I know full well that we are sometimes overlooked as long as we "perform." What I am trying to say is that our churches must be equipped with people who know what God has gifted them to do and operate in those gifts. My heart is for the health of our churches and I believe that is on God's heart. Please know that my intention is not to judge nor to offend simply to challenge and encourage my brothers and sisters in Christ.

If you don't remember anything I said in this book, remember this…

Follow God or

Love people

Obey His voice

Worship daily

Go with God and FLOW with God!

Confessions and Affirmations

Proverbs 12:14 (NIV) *From the fruit of their lips people are filled with good things, and the work of their hands brings them reward.* Confession is good for the soul. The more our ears hear a thing, the more our heart believes it and our actions follow it. Here's a peek a some of my daily confessions. Feel free to add confessions that are specific to your life.

<u>My Identity</u>

I recognize that I am a spirit. I have a soul. I live in a body. I worship in the Spirit. I walk in the Spirit. I pray in the Spirit. I live in the Spirit.

I trust in you, Lord, only because you are my hope and confidence.

I am growing in the things of God daily.

I have a hunger for the word of God and it is growing

everyday.

I deny myself today, take up my cross and follow you.

I am dressed in the full armor of God; the helmet of salvation, breastplate of righteousness, sword of the Spirit, shield of faith, belt of truth, shoes of peace that come the Gospel.

I declare that my ears are open and active to hear and obey the voice of the Lord.

I am walking everyday in courage and authority of God.

I have everything I need to do what God has called me to do.

I am in the most productive season of my life.

I have a keen sensitivity to God's voice and timing.

I am walking in newness; hearing new things, tasting new, seeing new things, experiencing new things. Everything is new.

I am walking in unlimited resources.

My Focus

Help me to hate my former life. I want to hate what you hate and love what you love.

Lord sit on the throne of my heart and take first priority.

My entire family is saved and filled with the Holy Ghost.

Light the flames of passion for what you have assigned my hands to do.

My future is secure and brighter than I could ever imagine.

Wasted time is being redeemed.

Remove scales from my eyes and open the eyes of my understanding.

The unusual favor of the Lord is upon me.

Release life-altering ideas and solutions to problems.

Expose what is hidden, reveal the secrets of men's hearts and tell me everything I need to know.

Release a word of knowledge, wisdom and prophecy today for friends family and foes.

<u>I'm Godly...</u>

I am a godly Wife/Husband.

I am a godly Mother/Father.

I am a godly Sister/Brother.

I am a godly Daughter/Son.

I am a godly Friend.

I am a godly Mentor.

I am a godly Visionary.

I am a godly Trailblazer

I am a godly Leader.

<u>I am's</u>

I am Focused.

I am Influential.

I am Bold.

I am Fearless.

I am Creative.

I am Disciplined.

I am Important.

I am Needed.

I am Impactful.

I have integrity.

I am Anointed.

I am Covered.

I am Honorable.

I am Humble.

I am Favored.

I am Powerful.

I am Extremely Prophetic.

I am Healthy.

I am Whole.

I am Healed.

I am Delivered.

I am Wealthy.

I am Discerning.

I am Wise.

I am Righteous.

I am Sanctified.

I am Holy.

Lord, I am Yours!

About the Author

Kristen D. Baker is an influential leader who produces music, conferences and community service events for professional and spiritual development. Known to go the extra mile to execute the will of the Lord, Kristen says, "Excellence is always in order." In her early years, she directed the award-winning Ridge View High Gospel Choir. Kristen earned her Bachelor of Science in Music with a concentration in vocal performance from Columbia College in Columbia, S.C.

After college, Kristen established two organizations: Kristen Baker Ministries and Perfect'd Praise LLC. Comprised of musicians, singers and dancers ages 16 to 26, the youth-led group hosts events to connect Christian, business, and civilian groups for fellowship and community building. In 2010, Kristen ed her first devotional, iHunger: Strengthen Your Connection with God in 21 Days. Kristen is an ordained minister and the Coordinator of Worship & Arts at Revealing Word Ministries under the leadership of Pastors Gary and Yasha Becton. She is committed to heralding the fact that God speaks and that are lives are exponentially better as a result of his voice. Kristen is also impacting the marketplace as a Kingdom-minded entrepreneur, as co-owner of MD Publications and a South Carolina realtor. Kristen's life motto is to blaze trails and build bridges!

www.ingramcontent.com/pod-product-compliance
Lightning Source LLC
Chambersburg PA
CBHW032131090426
42743CB00007B/551